AF279441

YOU TOO WILL KNOW ME

AMA ASANTEWA DIAKA

This is a work of fiction. All names, characters, places, and incidents are a product of the author's imagination. Any resemblance to real events or persons, living or dead, is entirely coincidental.

Published by Akashic Books
©2019 Ama Asantewa Diaka

ISBN: 978-1-61775-743-3

All rights reserved
Printed in China
First printing

Akashic Books
Brooklyn, New York, USA
Ballydehob, Co. Cork, Ireland
Twitter: @AkashicBooks
Facebook: AkashicBooks
E-mail: info@akashicbooks.com
Website: www.akashicbooks.com

African Poetry Book Fund
Prairie Schooner
University of Nebraska
110 Andrews Hall
Lincoln, Nebraska 68588

TABLE OF CONTENTS

PREFACE
by Tjawangwa Dema

Ama Asantewa Diaka's opening poem, "Paul's Whole verse," greets us with the words *"finally brethren,"* beginning with the presumption of a listener. But perhaps it is not a spectator that the poet conjures, but rather another presence, as do all prayers or confessions. Even the title of this collection, *You Too Will Know Me,* presumes an other and does so with an incisive language. The title's "too" points to a plurality beyond the self and possibly beyond many others. Yet, the knowing here is not reciprocal; instead, the reader will encounter personae quietly grappling with the politics of language—in particular, English—and the ways in which the acquisition of language is tied to power. The conjuring of a listener does not presume comprehension, but it does ask for engagement.

What follows is a series of poems that are "catechismal," swaying somewhere between conversation and confession. In this collection, Diaka not only employs word repetition, but also a call-and-response technique, even if the call is itself a rhetorical question and the answers to questions asked manifest in/as different poems. It may be, for example, that the question raised in "Spit": "what's the English word for someone who still has hope / in lovers who cause too much anxiety?" is answered in the poem "Suicide Sarah," about someone who loves a boy who is "always waiting / [...] / before he gives you all of his love . . ."

Diaka both interrogates and insists on the power of naming, allowing her to straddle what the anthropologist Anna Tsing calls stories that are both "true and fabulous." Diaka is unambiguous in her sense of place. She names not just Ghana, but, more specifically, Accra and Labadi. Likewise, no one is left to wonder if Ms. Atta could be Ms. Smith or Jones or otherwise; the poet's jollof is not merely rice, nor is it vaguely West African. Diaka claims it and files it—not unexpectedly for some readers—under *"whatever things are noble."*

In her opening poem, Diaka already shows that, though she is invested in listeners, she is not interested in explaining herself to cultural outsiders. "The lover born on a Thursday" would turn at the sound of that phrase as though s/he/they had been tapped on the shoulder and called by name, but to anyone unfamiliar with Ghanaian naming practices the words may appear to hold music but not meaning. The poet must hold both thoughts at once—specificity and the myth of the universal, invitation and boundary, telling and listening. Here is Diaka sweeping her eye both inward and outwards, and interrogating the limitations of language:

> I have hit a roadblock in trying to use language to navigate my feelings.
> the same words that pave way, stand in my way.
> how do I distract myself from myself in order to free myself?
> how do I use language against itself?

These are poems that make no bones about their desire to bear witness. Diaka is utilizing empathy's ability to make the very specific resonate. In paying homage to the most ordinary of things—from the porridge seller's smile, to the way a stranger's "laughter tumbles down like the hollow echo of a djembe"—the work suggests that, even if the beautiful ones are not yet born, we need not be complicit in turning away from the ones with the "unpretty laugh" or the ones who are "not what the world would label as pretty," and who in turn are paid their pensions late. Diaka's restraint is shown in her avoiding of preachiness. Instead, the poems remain as prayer, as confessional.

While the reading of poetry is often a sedentary act, the eye encounters poetry differently from the rest of the body. Does it not embody motion, moving across lines and space and often backwards in an attempt to further apprehend meaning or music? Profanity in poetry, however, is a door that swings both ways: to draw the eye or to repel it. And here we have a poet working earnestly to find her place between the gratuitous and the necessary. We begin to trust that she knows what necessitates placing the word "blowjobs" three lines after the word "God," as we watch her grapple to refocus the eye when the lyrics change to a chorus of "everybody" and "Damn" until we are left with

> Damn everybody!
> Do they not know
> [. . .]
> There's something about you
> that makes looking away impossible.

Throughout this collection, the body sags and is praised; it decays, which "is not always synonymous to rot." Its various limbs, organs, and fluids unravel—feet, molars, spit, and more connect what is otherwise an unorthodox assemblage of writings on love. All poets have their preoccupations and Diaka certainly has no shortage of them. But she is also invested in candour and attuned to precarity; not just the material but the ways in which we attempt to rationalize pleasure, anxiety, labor, faith, as well as gendered and racialized inequality.

> I'm reminded you are still
> a sharp, blooming, flustered, selfish, reckless, gooey boy
> I love—who has no desire to learn
>
> > to love me back in a language I understand.

There is a forthrightness to many of these poems, which is to say the poems say what they mean to say. But there is music, too, that "stands out / like a nipple on a cold rainy night." "Bloom," for example, is characterized by the use of quick rhythms and sharply drawn vignettes, as in a neatly spliced together silent film-cum-documentary you want to watch over and over again.

The terms "new" and "emerging" can be thrown about loosely to refer to poets whose voices are new to *us*. Admittedly, these terms can allow a poet precious room for development, but can also hold one in perceived stasis. So, let us be clear: Diaka begins *anew* here on the page after years of performing and recording and engaging with audiences. But as Diaka's poems clearly demonstrate, "newness" is certainly not a measure of talent.

> I have been fretting over things that God shakes his head at
> toying with faith as if it were a disappearing act.
> One minute I'm full of it,
> the next, I don't exactly know the shape of it.
> I fret over now and tomorrow,
> giving myself and God a headache.
> Spoon feed myself faith,
> and come up hungry again.

Here is a poet whose practiced weaving of talk and song is a testament to her devotion to language and her clarity of vision. Those of us who have encountered Diaka with excitement invite you to listen with us as she offers us a new song, one which will surely not be her last.